The Platinum Rule and Other Contrarian Sayings

To order additional copies, please contact us.
BookSurge, LLC
www.booksurge.com
1-866-308-6235
orders@booksurge.com

The Platinum Rule and Other Contrarian Sayings

The First 60 Years

Tuchy Palmieri

2006

The Platinum Rule and Other Contrarian Sayings

Dedication: "To the makers of Salada Tea, for their helpful sayings during the early years of my life. To my children Kathleen, Phil, and John, whose love kept me going through the dark years. To my Dad, Mom, aunts, and uncles who filled my head with time-tested sayings and anecdotes. And most of all to my lovely wife, Susan, who has raised me up to heights I have never known and did not know existed. Her love, encouragement, and support are second to none."

The Platinum Rule and Other Contrarian Sayings

The First 60 Years

1) Our standard of thinking either raises or lowers our standard of living.

2) The battle of life is won when you leave the battle and both your friends and your enemies regret it.

3) Birth is but a rung on the ladder of life.

4) Death is but a rung on the ladder of life.

5) The sobering reality is that no matter how far or how high you climb the mountain, you must eventually come down.

6) Challenges and opportunities go hand in hand.

7) Problems and opportunities go hand in hand.

8) The question is not whether or not a person is lazy, but rather what is he lazy about.

9)   Friendliness and courtesy are free. Use them generously.

10)   Often I walk through life with a candle in one hand and a match in the other, and rely on the light of others to guide my way.

11)   The real measure of hard work is accomplishment.

12)   The gates of success swing on the hinges of action and persistence.

13)   Today the cost of communication is high, but the cost of not communicating is even higher.

14)   Life works.

15)   For me, wisdom gets the credit when fear has earned it.

16)   Some people state opinions as facts, some people state facts as opinions, and still others have an opinion about the facts.

17)   To make a mistake and learn from it is progression, to make the same mistake over and over is obsession.

18)   Life's real treasures cannot be found beneath the ocean, nor buried in the sand. They can only be found by opening the heart. And the key that opens this treasure chest is the key of love.

19)   While it is true that you can win a battle and lose the war it is equally true that you cannot win the war without winning a battle.

20)   To see properly one must open the mind before opening the eyes.

21)   Often the miracle of life is seen through death.

22)   Sometimes one must lose to win.

23)   Often I choose blindness over the pain of vision; thus I kill the possibility of joy of the newfound experience.

24)   For every exception there is a rule.

25)   It is far better to do and not know than it is to know and not <u>do.</u>

26)   As strange as it seems, when you listen you will be heard.

27)   Some people know a lot about a little, some people know a little about a lot, and others know a little about a little and say a lot about a lot.

28)   The man who searches for the ends of the earth will search forever.

29)   An ounce of intention is worth more than a pound of manure.

30) The bridge of success is actually built upon the foundation of failure.

31) Be grateful for failures as they make success possible.

32) Sometimes right can be wrong.

33) I'm patiently impatient.

34) We use a mirror to reflect the outer world and we use our imagination to reflect our inner world.

35) The mathematics of love has just addition and multiplication.

36) Reaching out to someone lengthens your reach.

37) Money talks; however, sometimes it whispers.

38) The only thing I can give another is I.

39) After you prioritize your priorities, prioritize your actions.

40) Love is seeing with your heart and not with your eyes.

41) An upset is something you do to yourself; a setup is something that is done to you.

42) Sometimes the quickest way to stop communications is to start talking.

43) On the highway of life you must often change directions to get where you are going.

44) It does no good to open the door if you fail to step through it.

45) Talk is cheap, except when you go back on your word.

46) While time waits for no man, life waits for no time.

47) Add an "o" to "god" and you get "good;" take the "d" from "devil" and you get "evil."

48) The most precious gifts you receive are not found in gift-wrapped boxes.

49) Think big but also act bigger.

50) Swimming with the current does not work if that is not the direction you need to go.

51) Real beauty starts at the skin and goes deep.

52) Sometimes going backwards is necessary before one can move forward.

53) Yesterday's impossibility becomes today's possibility and tomorrow's destiny.

54) Some have so little and care so much; others have so much and care so little.

55) Most stories are untold.

56) When you are up the creek without a paddle it's far better to be up the creek without a paddle going down, than to be down the creek going up.

57) There is no division in the mathematics of love.

58) The real winner wins even when he loses, and the real loser loses even when he wins.

59) The lessons of life are not found in a neatly bound book.

60) The lessons of life are found in the book of experience.

61) Love is accepting each other in sanity and madness.

62) Beauty, like diamonds, has many facets.

63) The surest way to get people behind you is by getting in line.

64) The toughest prison to escape from is the one that has no fences or walls.

65) Often what makes things work is work.

66)　Spring is nature's fireworks.

67)　Experience---failure over time.

68)　It matter not how precious the metal is that binds you.

69)　The only person who it is appropriate to possess is oneself, yet we often reject ourselves.

70)　Laughter is a way of communicating in any language.

71)　Wrong makes right, right.

72)　An opportunity that does not come at the right time is not an opportunity, but a problem disguised as an opportunity.

73)　Do not blindly follow another's road to success as his road is under construction.

74)　The ability to hold on is a good character trait, but so is the ability to let go.

75)　"Justice" is when we are all treated equally in an unjust way.

76)　To complete something you must first start it.

77)　The only way to finish something is to start it.

78) For greater happiness some of us must learn to play at work and work at play.

79) It's not how you look through another person's eyes, but rather how you look through your own that is important.

80) Taking a step up is not always the appropriate thing to do.

81) An hour of joy is shorter than an hour of pain.

82) All that comes with the bill of rights is the bill of wrongs.

83) One must first succeed at failing before one can succeed at succeeding.

84) We must take the time to make the time.

85) There is no deed so bad that it cannot be interpreted by someone as being good, and no deed so good that it cannot be interpreted as being bad.

86) A man without a plan has "plan inaction."

87) In death people disappear from view only to be seen more clearly by the heart.

88) The best instruction that is given is when, as a result of giving the instruction, the teacher learns something.

89) Thoughts change; people don't.

90) To succeed at nothing is the ultimate failure.

91) Love is knowing what buttons to push and not pushing them.

92) The free are often imprisoned and the imprisoned are often free.

93) Having something of value taken away from you can be a great gift.

94) Death cures all ills.

95) "Success" is found in the dictionary between "determination" and "work."

96) Time is one of the most precious things one can possess, and yet more often than not one is possessed by time.

97) The people who say you can have only 24 hours in a day obviously did not fly from London to New York.

98) Life-- that span of time between birth and death.

99) The more I try to save it, spend it, schedule it, master it, the more I realize I am possessed by it-- time.

100) It is strange in life that less can be more and more can be less.

101) The path of success and the path of failure are often the same; the only difference is one's willingness to continue.

102) I have learned the secret of life-- it goes by.

103) The gravest failure of all may be one's failure to fail.

104) Some people are so busy climbing the mountain of life that they miss the peace in the valley.

105) Every man has his challenge, but not every man knows what his challenge is.

106) Even with pain there is comfort.

107) Being a man is difficult, and becoming a man is a lifelong process.

108) Teach yourself before you teach others.

109) To know is good; to understand is better, and to believe is best.

110) I have found that in life the master is often the servant and the servant the master.

111) If you do not live your life your life will live you.

112) Some of our best speakers do not communicate.

113) A successful person fails until he succeeds, and a failure succeeds until he fails.

114) I don't know what's worse, solving the right problem the wrong way, or solving the wrong problem the right way.

115) The time to check for toilet paper is before you sit down.

116) We all are sculptors of our lives.

117) Our lives are like clay, which can be molded by us, and shaped as time goes on.

118) Dying for your loved ones can be a great act. Living for them can be an even greater act.

119) Many say that growth occurs through the years. I say that growth occurs in the time between pain and pleasure.

120) If at first you succeed, say a prayer and smile.

121) We can be wrong most of the time and win, and we can be right most of the time and lose.

122) It's not what lovers see in each other that makes their relationship work, it's what they do not see in each other that makes it work.

123) He who hesitates is found.

124) When the babe in the woods sees the woods he's no longer a babe.

125) When life throws you a curveball, step up to the plate and hit a home run.

126) Yesterday's pillar is but today's stepping stone.

127) Isn't it strange that most of us spend our lives trying to get back to the way we were when we were born?

128) No matter whom or what I try to control, I find that I'm in fact controlled by them or by that.

129) Often there is gain with loss and loss with gain.

130) I'm too busy holding on to the past and reaching for the future to enjoy the present.

131) I seek to control the uncontrollable; while I do this, the controllable goes uncontrolled.

132) In every success there is a failure.

133)   The only thing made to take crap is the toilet.

134)   Failure-- not trying again.

135)   All men are wise and all men are foolish. To make them one or the other, just change the subject matter.

136)   Par for the course is better than par as most people do not get par.

137)   A key to successful living-- enjoy life, as it is yours to do with as you please.

138)   We are all taking the same path; we just start at different points.

139)   Some hills are older than others and some hills are unborn.

140)   Every man is born deaf, dumb, and blind.

141)   Every man chooses his deafness, dumbness, and blindness.

142)   I'm very selective. I'm selective about my thinking, memory, and listening.

143)   Do not pity the deaf, dumb, and blind as they did not choose that, but pity those of us who have chosen to be deaf, dumb, and blind.

144)   I have risked, I have lost, and then I have won.

145)   I asked-- I received. I feared-- I lost.

146)   Fear is but an opportunity to be courageous.

147)   The right word is worth more than a thousand pictures.

148)   It does no good for your ship to come in if it's void of cargo.

149)   One need only to attend a business meeting to know that talk is not cheap.

150)   It does no good to walk the straight and narrow path if the path is the wrong one or if you are going in the wrong direction.

151)   The lesson I have to learn is that I have lessons to learn.

152)   The greatest illusion in life is to believe that you have no illusions.

153)   If your ship does not come in, go to a different port.

154)   Knowledge brings appreciation and lack of it brings fear.

155) It's not the answers to the questions you ask that are important, but rather the questions you ask to have answered.

156) All healing starts with the four words, "I am roached up."

157) Some people speak for their words while others have their words speak for them.

158) In life it is not doing the right thing, nor in doing things right that is important, what's important is doing the right things right.

159) If you do not schedule your week it will schedule you.

160) When there is peace within there are no battles without.

161) True peace comes when we stop the battle within and surrender.

162) The toughest peace negotiation is the one with yourself.

163) Smart men do dumb things.

164) It matters not how many tears one sheds, what matters is that the tears shed be shed after the loss has been acknowledged.

165) Sometimes the greatest gift someone can give is no present at all.

166) When all else fails, reread the instructions.

167) More often than not the truth about yourself comes from the lips of others.

168) To my amazement I have often found that it is out of one's weakness that real strength stems.

169) The occurrence of an event brings neither joy nor sorrow. It's one's knowledge and interpretation that brings the joy or sorrow.

170) Often I find that my tears are shed after an event rather than concurrent with it.

171) Often I am in such a hurry to start a "new" that I do not stop to complete the old.

172) When you are sad about something ending, remember that you cannot start if you are still going.

173) Later does not exist.

174) Great sinners make great saints.

175) To change others, change yourself.

176) I hear silence.

177)   To hear silence you must not hear.

178)   There is a condition when the deaf can hear and the hearing are deaf-- the deaf hear silence and the hearing, to hear silence, must not hear.

179)   A cripple can stand head and shoulders above men who walk.

180)   Live and unlearn.

181)   You have to be at bat in order to strike out.

182)   Unlearning a lesson is harder than learning it.

183)   Sometimes the best way to hang on is to let go.

184)   We are all alcoholics; it just depends on what you get drunk on.

185)   The free may be imprisoned and the imprisoned may be free.

186)   Having something of value taken away from you can be a great gift.

187)   To see something or someone better often requires moving away from that something or someone.

188)   Laughter is a way of communicating in every language.

189)   Some have so little and care so much and others have so much and care so little.

190)   The small difference between an "aw shit" and an "attaboy" is almost immeasurable.

191)   It is often said that love is blind. I say that love sees so clearly that it goes beyond the surface to the beauty within.

192)   If you walk in a straight line long enough and far enough two things will happen-- you will end up where you started and you will have walked in a circle.

193)   Memories are to be made and not lived.

194)   I forgive others to better forgive myself.

195)   We use the mirror to reflect our outer world and our imagination to reflect our inner world.

196)   I look but I cannot see for I suffer from the severest blindness of all.

197)   It really does not matter if you are barking up the wrong tree, you will get the same result.

198)   You cannot possess anything without it possessing you.

199) The question is, do I walk the dog or does the dog walk me?

200) Time tames all men.

201) Life is not good for you; if you are exposed to it long enough you will die.

202) Warning: Life is hazardous to your health. It has been proven that prolonged exposure is fatal.

203) The real weightlifter exercises the muscles of his mind.

204) It takes all my strength to be gentle.

205) One of the best ways to lighten your load is to lighten yourself.

206) In dealing with children all parents are fools.

207) To overcome a difficulty, find a bigger one and work on it.

208) One of the surest ways to break something is to fix something that worked.

209) Getting points doesn't matter if you are not playing the game.

210) You are really communicating when you are answering the unspoken questions.

211) Problems create opportunities and opportunities create problems.

212) If a reason is good enough we use it as an excuse.

213) A good reason is your best excuse.

214) We are all composers in the symphony of life.

215) No one can let you down if you have your feet on the ground.

216) Remember, when you are sitting on the fence you are not going anywhere.

217) When deciding, your first decision is to decide.

218) The person who never retreats will never win.

219) Pain is a forceful speaker, and yet many of us do not listen.

220) When pain speaks we listen.

221) The body has many voices, most of which speak very quietly so we must learn to listen to them.

222) Love is more than one thing. That is why it is so hard to define. It's friendship and trust in action.

223)   The more I try to find time, the more time I lose.

224)   I consume so much energy trying to save time that I must rest, and more often than not I use all the time I saved.

225)   A woman who tends to her man, tends to herself.

226)   The surest way to get people to change is for you to change.

227)   Lemon de la lemon.

228)   No one ever got lost by following his or her heart.

229)   Whenever I get discouraged about the slow progress I am making, I think of the diamond and the slow progress it made changing from carbon.

230)   Some people are like diamonds; they improve under pressure. Others are like eggs-- they crack.

231)   Life is like a river with its twists and turns, and like the river, life flows ever onward towards its destination.

232)   The luckiest drunk is the one who is drunk on life.

233)   Alimony- when it hurts to give up.

234)   Silence-- often it is the most eloquent form of communication and at times it is the severest form of criticism.

235)   When traveling down a path we often forget that we can choose to change paths or to make new ones.

236)   Problems solve problems and upon solving problems, new and different problems are created.

237)   Truthfulness-- love in action.

238)   The main ingredients in love are trust and truthfulness.

239)   It makes little sense to knock on the door when you are inside and it makes less sense standing outside waiting for the knock of opportunity.

240)   Two captains sink a ship.

241)   When in doubt, ask.

242)   Knowledge without action is like a rose without a stem.

243)   If you are doing what you like it really doesn't matter where you are doing it.

244)   Everyone appreciates beauty; the difference lies in our appreciation of what beauty is.

245)   Often it is better to have nothing with an opportunity than to have something without it.

246)   Dynamic integrity—when the degree of integrity changes to suit the situation.

247)   The golden age—now.

248)   Women are like fruit-- some are bitter, some are sweet; some are soft and others are firm, and as fruit they come in all sizes and shapes.

249)   A candle unlit is but wax and string; once lit, however, it lights the world.

250)   The problem with following in someone's footsteps is that you must stop when they do.

251)   To overtake you must first undertake.

252)   The war amongst men has not stopped; we have just put down the sword for the tongue.

253)   The tongue is mightier than the pen.

254)   Many say that when you get older you start to lose your sight; I say that you just exchange it for a vision that is far greater.

255)   To unlock the door, just turn the key.

256)   We are always preparing; some of us prepare to succeed, others prepare to fail.

257)   We cannot choose the peaks and valleys in our lives. What we can choose are the paths we use to climb the peaks and travel through the valleys.

258)   There is one thing stronger than the mightiest force and more powerful than all the world's wealth. It is one who is inspired.

259)   Some people use money; others let money use them.

260)   Retreat-- moving forward backwards.

261)   One cannot say yes to something without saying no to something else.

262)   In failure there is success. In foolishness there is wisdom.

263)   Judge a man not by the mistakes he makes but by how he reacts to his mistakes.

264)   Success stands on the foundation of failure. Failure stands on the foundation of failure.

265)   Even blind men can see eye to eye.

266)   Man's most significant growth is not between birth and age 12 as is most commonly believed; rather it is in the years between children and grandchildren when our most significant growth occurs.

267)   Many truths are location dependent.

268)   Real beauty is more than skin deep.

269)   Many times my brightest days are when it's cloudy or dark outside.

270)   In weakness there is strength and in strength there is weakness; the willow and the mighty oak demonstrate this in a storm.

271)   Communication is the art of making the impossible possible.

272)   One of the reasons a person does not answer the knock of opportunity is because he or she is not listening.

273)   Often it seems that when the body is strong one is weak spiritually, and when the body is weak one is strong spiritually.

274)   Often the very thing that makes you strong makes you weak; also the very thing that makes you weak is the very thing that makes you strong.

275)   The truth is not achieved by facts alone.

276)   It matters not how big or small you are; what matters is how big or small you are in relation to others.

277)   We were given two ears and two eyes so that we can see and hear four times more than we speak.

278)   For every saying and proverb there is an opposite saying or proverb that is as valid.

279)   Often the truth is sweet and a lie is bitter.

280)   All truths need not be bitter.

281)   Love remains the most powerful medicine on earth.

282)   Some things have to be believed to be seen.

283)   We are either producing results or producing justifications.

284)   Setting the limits in the form of stops is what allows the bus to work.

285)   Three is a crowd, unless you are a Mormon.

286)   It matters not how often we stumble, but in which way we stumble.

287)   Do not be discouraged if you stumble because if you stumble you are moving and if you stumble forward you are progressing.

288)   God grant me the courage to stumble. If I do then I know I'm growing.

289)   It can be said that our lives are like water in a river. We continue down the river of life until we reach the end of the river, where we merge with a greater body.

290)   No need to go an extra mile when a meter will do.

291)   I find that you can keep your eye on the ball and not see it.

292)   Nature treats all men equally.

293)   It does no good to keep your eye on the ball if you keep your mind on something else.

294)   Am I a byproduct of a product, which is a byproduct of a product?

295)   Often the truth hurts, but it is more painful to lie.

296)   "Possibility" can be found in the dictionary between "courage" and "willingness."

297)   On any journey you reach a point when you are no longer going but are coming.

298)   To find out if you are coming or going you must figure out how far you have gone and how far you have left.

299)   If you keep going long enough, you will start coming.

300)   Out of chaos comes order and out of order comes chaos.

301)   Some talk is very expensive.

302)   Quality is important today because there is a tomorrow.

303)   No man is free who is not the master of himself.

304)   To master others, master yourself.

305)   No lawyer is better than a bad lawyer.

306)   There is no rule like an old rule.

307)   Make your life a statement, not a question.

308)   What are you building with the lumber of your life?

309) All time is not equal.

310) Failure succeeds first.

311) If you feel screwed up just unscrew yourself.

312) It is a problem not to have problems.

313) Your speaking whispers when compared to action.

314) Speech whispers; action roars.

315) Being good includes being bad.

316) Some possibilities are impossible and some impossibilities are possible.

317) Everybody loves quality.

318) Some people work hard at working and others work hard at resting.

319) To understand that one misunderstands is a great step towards wisdom.

320) It is a mistake to view a mistake as being bad.

321) Don't bother looking for a pear under an apple tree.

322) The first step in learning is confusion.

323) If you do not follow directions then the directions will follow you.

324) If you pick someone else up you must also pick yourself up.

325) Love is a commitment that requires one to de-commit in favor of the commitment.

326) I can only know you to the degree that I know me.

327) What I say governs what I do.

328) Even a jackass knows it is better to pull than to push.

329) I not only want the path to be clearly marked but I also want it to be easy to follow.

330) The path of life is not straight or level; it has its twists and turns, it rises and dips, and has obstacles that must be overcome.

331) Most people are satisfied with their unsatisfaction.

332) Just because the path is straight and narrow does not mean it's the right one for you to take.

333) What is life? It's everything; without it you have nothing.

334)   Knowing something about something keeps you from knowing more about something.

335)   When you know that something isn't possible then it's impossible, and when you don't know that something is impossible then it is possible.

336)   While driving down the highway of life many people lose their brakes.

337)   Being out on a limb often isn't enough. A limb can be so thick that there is no risk.

338)   Palmieri's second law: You cannot lie about the truth; you can only lie about a lie.

339)   We gather knowledge to learn; once gathered we know, and upon knowing we stop gathering information, which keeps us from knowing.

340)   Life depends upon life.

341)   A marriage goes through phases like the moon; there is the new moon, the honeymoon, the blue moon, and the full moon.

342)   If I were a bird my goal would be to hatch myself everyday.

343)   I am no longer concerned if I am on the right track; I am concerned if I am going in the right direction.

344)   It's far better to be washed up than washed out.

345)   It's not just the cream that rises to the top.

346)   Some people have strong wills; others have strong won'ts.

347)   To learn we must forget; forgetting is a part of learning.

348)   Just because it's cloudy does not mean that the sun is not shining.

349)   It matters not that your life goes by quickly or not; it matters that it goes by.

350)   Be grateful that life goes by quickly for you; that means you are enjoying it. Just ask the person who is in pain if life goes by quickly.

351)   Success: failure to fail.

352)   I have failed enough to succeed.

353)   Many people on easy street do not believe it's easy.

354)   Easy Street can be found between Action Road and Dedication Avenue.

355)   Truth is shorter than fiction.

356) While it is true that the pen is mightier than the sword, it is also true that the tongue is mightier than the pen.

357) Getting on a train is a start; getting on the train that is on the right track is progress, and getting on the train going in the right direction is success.

358) Where there is a will there is no argument.

359) We are all strong and all weak; it just depends upon the situation.

360) Fight fire with water.

361) Even comparing apples against apples does no good unless you take into consideration the different varieties.

362) In life you may not be able to choose the mountains you must climb, but you can choose the paths you will take to climb them.

363) Love is the fertilizer in the garden of life.

264) Success stands on the shoulders of failure.

365) Results are like icebergs-- mostly under the surface and not visible.

366) We are blind to our blindness and deaf to our deafness.

367)   Just because things add up does not mean they are right.

368)   One thing many people do not realize about bills is that they created them and often it is their choice to continue them.

369)   Time, like money, can be spent foolishly or wisely.

370)   The real winners in life do not beat anyone but rather help others to win.

371)   Without strings the bikini would not work.

372)   The extraordinary comes from the ordinary, and the ordinary comes from the extraordinary.

373)   Seasons are seasonal and they are regional.

374)   A problem with meeting people halfway is that peoples' definitions of "halfway" are different.

375)   If you approach the relationship with the notion of 50-50 you will get 50 percent; if you approach it with the notion of 100 percent you will get 100 percent.

376)   Beauty does not exist without love.

377)   The busy person always has time to be busy.

378) Some learn slowly, some learn later and some learn never.

379) The one good thing about having a bad day or a bad week is that it is in the past.

380) You cannot always follow the path of another as your journey is different.

381) To find a needle in the haystack, just remove the hay from the stack.

382) In the mathematics of love things do not have to add up.

383) Benefits do not exist without a cost.

384) Everybody's always going through something.

385) Friendship: the cornerstone in the foundation of life.

386) Some people will not rock the boat even when it is sinking.

387) Yesterday's weakness is today's strength.

388) We speak best when we say nothing at all.

389) Silence speaks louder than words.

390) A reason we find insights rare is because they are out of sight.

391) The right tool used the wrong way is not any better than the wrong tool used the right way. Sometimes the wrong tool used the right way will get you the results you need.

392) It matters not how many times we stumble, but how often we get up and in which direction we stumble.

393) If you really want to be heard, speak silently.

394) Deroach yourself.

395) The best way to get experience is to do it.

396) It seems that many people believe that getting to the point is a painful experience.

397) Do you make money, or does money make you?

398) Sometimes to see something requires you to be blind to something else.

399) It is through blindness that we see.

400) It is the little people who are big enough to make you successful.

401) Many people worship the man who has all the answers, even if the answers are wrong.

402) People do not get upset when you make a mistake; they get upset when you don't do anything about the mistake.

403)   Let me fail today so that I may succeed tomorrow.

404)   The best way to happiness is in making more of the things you do be the things that make you happy.

405)   Have the things you must do be the things that make you happy, then you are guaranteed happiness.

406)   If you are moving ahead and you stumble, you are at least stumbling forward.

407)   There is no such thing as a bad penny.

408)   When words fail, silence speaks.

409)   To profit one must participate.

410)   Success comes from failing a different way until you fail to fail.

411)   More often than not the very thing we fear is the very thing that when pursued brings one fulfillment.

412)   The only time I stop is when I fear fear.

413)   Often we are so busy looking we do not see.

414)   Whatever you have has you.

415)   One man's necessity is another man's luxury.

416)   We are all addicts; what we are addicted to is the only thing that differs.

417)   Often it is the very things that we like that hurt us.

418)   The gamble without risk is the biggest gamble of all.

419)   Fifty percent of the people listen but do not hear; the other fifty percent hear but do not listen.

420)   Living life without asking for help is one step above not living at all.

421)   When speaking, all too often we choose our words for their acceptability, rather than for their accuracy.

422)   The lock gives the key meaning.

423)   You succeed when you fail to fail.

424)   If at first you do not succeed you are normal.

425)   As we get older we think that we are losing our vision. Quite the contrary; we exchange it for vision that is more encompassing.

426)   I know of no blessing that does not have within it a problem and I know of no problem that does not have within it a blessing.

427)   You are as great as you allow yourself to be.

428)   The successful person allows himself to fail.

429)   The difference between an acquaintance and a friend: an acquaintance gives advice; a friend gives himself.

430)   Most people not only want the world, they want it for free.

431)   If you grind your ax too often you will eventually lose it.

432)   The advantage a plain-looking woman has is that her appearance does not prevent people from seeing her beauty.

433)   Sometimes nothing is better than something, especially if that something is bad.

434)   Not all scars can be seen.

435)   In some cases it's much easier to tie the knot than to untie it.

436)   Generalizations are general.

437) Walk another mile; often walking a mile is not enough.

438) Judge a man by his performances, not his promises.

439) We are all gems; different, yet of equal value.

440) We are all diamonds with different facets.

441) The size of the hole is no indication of the size of the clam.

442) While it may be true that it is better to give than to receive, to receive may be the best gift that you can give.

443) You are your thoughts.

444) Just because your head is above water doesn't mean that you are close to shore.

445) Sometimes the wisest thing to say is, "I don't know."

446) Sometimes the wisest thing to do is nothing.

447) Life is made of contradictions; contradicted by contradictions.

448) The most important relationship to have is with yourself.

449)   A fault is a virtue.

450)   Treat yourself as you would treat others.

451)   Love is a word worth a thousand pictures.

452)   Don't buy at the low or sell at the high.

453)   We are all beginners.

454)   Persistence is the foundation of education.

455)   Palmieri's law: laws keep changing.

456)   Beauty is international.

457)   Never eat a peacock.

458)   Sometimes the best lesson to learn is that there is no lesson to learn.

459)   Language cares not what one's status is.

460)   Failure is just the first step on the pathway of success.

461)   Sometimes the fastest way to get to an eastern destination is to take a western route.

462)   For every rose there are dozens of thorns.

463)   The thorns protect the rose.

464) You may not be able to teach an old dog new tricks, but an old dog can teach a new dog old tricks.

465) The point I often try to make is that there is no point.

466) It's the flaw that makes the diamond precious.

467) Everything that starts, ends.

468) It's tough to make a point with a dull mind.

469) The experience we learn from need not be our own.

470) We are all alone together.

471) Who coaches the coach?

472) Your weakness is your strength.

473) Sometimes our vision prevents us from seeing clearly.

474) There is a Samson in every man and a Delilah in every woman.

475) There are more wealthy poor people than there are wealthy rich people.

476) Sometimes what I see blocks my vision.

477)   While it is true that there are two sides there is also a middle.

478)   There are no good guys and no bad guys.

479)   We are all poor and all rich.

480)   All wisdom begins with ignorance; all ignorance does not end with wisdom.

481)   Ignorance is the father of wisdom.

482)   Perfection does not exist; what's perfect becomes imperfect.

483)   The oak demonstrates that there is weakness in strength.

484)   Your closest neighbor may be the furthest away.

485)   The fountain of youth is found within.

486)   My enemy, my friend, myself.

487)   As a general rule you must be wrong before you can be right.

488)   I'm a collection of experiences and memories.

489)   Everyone has at least one bad bone.

490) The success of your internal marriage determines the success of your external marriage.

491) Can anyone afford a free ride?

492) I have conquered all except myself.

493) What we see with our hearts is without color; it cannot see the color of evil and hate.

494) Words can move mountains and destroy nations.

495) The real wise man is someone who knows when not to use his brain.

496) Seeing is a matter of choice even for the blind person.

497) Pain does not discriminate.

498) I have the answer-- sometimes it is not appropriate to get the answer.

499) My desire to understand sometimes stops me from action so that I can understand.

500) We all have blemishes, but all blemishes cannot be seen.

501) Honesty is a matter of degree and is based upon perception.

502)   Most of us want the plum and do not want the pit, and yet it is the pit that will keep us eating plums.

503)   Palmieri's postulate: the line you are not in moves faster and as soon as you change lines, the other one moves faster.

504)   What you see determines how you feel and how you feel determines what you see.

505)   Life is a lesson.

506)   Sometimes to be in hot water is not bad.

507)   For things to work in life you must work.

508)   The mind limits the body and the body limits the mind.

509)   We are our blemishes.

510)   We are what we are not.

511)   The reason sitting on the fence is so hard is that it is narrow, and it's often pointed.

512)   Forgiveness is the eraser that wipes the slate clean.

513)   The good thing about falling when you are climbing down the mountain is that you are going in the right direction.

514) You cannot stumble if you do not move.

515) People who do not trip or stumble are not moving.

516) Don't worry about the money; it will disappear over time.

517) Sitting on the fence can be painful and uncomfortable.

518) Often one must go through hell to reach Heaven.

519) Fear and frustration are the parents of anger.

520) The platinum rule: do unto others as they would have you do unto them.

521) A fool knows how wise he is; a wise man knows how foolish he is.

522) The cost of saving is often more than the saving.